Learning About Mammals

BY

DEBBIE ROUTH

COPYRIGHT © 2002 Mark Twain Media, Inc.

ISBN 1-58037-191-4

Printing No. CD-1537

Mark Twain Media, Inc., Publishers
Distributed by Carson-Dellosa Publishing Company, Inc.

Table of Contents

Introduction

Welcome to a series of books devoted to the *Chordata* Phyla. A **chordate** is an animal that has a **vertebrate**, (backbone). Every animal in the animal kingdom can be subdivided into two main groups. The **invertebrates** (without a backbone) make up 95 percent of all the known animals. The **vertebrates** (with a backbone) make up only five percent of the animal kingdom. The vertebrates are then subdivided even further into seven classes: the three classes of fish, amphibians, reptiles, birds, and mammals. This book is devoted to a diversified group of animals called **mammals**, also known as class *mammalia*.

Mammals live in a wide range of habitats and are the most diversified class of vertebrates. Do you know what diversified means? **Diversified** means that vertebrates are varied in their structures, largely due to their adaptability to their habitats. Organisms must be well suited to their environment, or they could not survive where they live. Due to specialized adaptations, mammals have a wonderful ability to live and survive everywhere. Mammals may be very diversified, but they still have many traits or characteristics in common. Student observers will use many scientific process skills throughout this series. The reinforcement sheets that follow the lessons contain at least one higher-level thinking question. So, student observers, put on those thinking caps and use your process skills to observe, classify, analyze, debate, design, and report. This unit contains a variety of lessons that will help you practice scientific processes as you discover all about mammals. Come on, student observers, let's use our critical thinking skills to take a closer look at the world of mammals.

* **Teacher note:** Each lesson opens with a manageable amount of text for the student to read. The succeeding pages contain exercises and illustrations that are varied and plentiful. Phonetic spellings and simple definitions for terms are also included to assist the student. The lessons may be used as a complete unit for the entire class or as supplemental material for the reluctant learner. The tone of the book is informal; a dialogue is established between the book and the student.

What Is a Mammal?: *Definition*

Kingdom: *Animalia*
  Phylum: *Chordata*
    Subphylum: *Vertebrata*
      Class: *Mammalia*

    Hello, student observers! Today, we are going to take a closer look at a group of complex vertebrates, the mammals. Mammals are the conquerors of the earth. Some scientists believe that all modern mammals came from animals called *Therapsids* (THER-up-sidz). The early mammals did not have to compete for food or living space after the dinosaurs died out. The mammals survived, reproduced, and became the most successful group of animals.

    Fossils show us that mammals are the **newest** animals on the earth. The main characteristics of this new class of animals are:

    Mammals have a **spine** (backbone), which is made up of small bones called **vertebrae**. They have a **notochord** (nerve cord) that runs along the spine, connecting it to the skull.

    Mammals have hair on their bodies at some time during their lives. Many have fur that traps air and helps keep them warm. Others have very little hair and rely on fat under their skin to keep them warm.

    Mammals are **endothermic** (warm-blooded), meaning their body temperature remains the same regardless of the surrounding air or water.

    Mammals have **mammary glands** that produce milk so mothers can nurse their young. Mammals take much better care of their young in comparison to other animals. One kind of mammal, the **marsupial**, carries its young with it in a little pouch. Most mammals give birth to live **offspring** (their young).

    Mammals have a complex brain; they have skulls that protect large **cerebrums** (thinking centers). Mammals are the most intelligent animals. Man is the most intelligent mammal.

    Mammals have **special teeth** depending on the type of food they eat. The shape of its teeth tells us about the food an animal eats. These teeth help the mammal digest its food quickly, thus giving it a quick energy boost. This makes mammals more active than reptiles, which are sluggish for a week or two after they swallow their prey whole.

    As you can see, observers, to say a mammal is a warm-blooded, air-breathing, milk-producing vertebrate that has hair is definitely an understatement!

Name:_____ Date: _____

What Is a Mammal?: *Reinforcement Activity*

To the student observer: On this worksheet, show what you know about mammals.

I.   Fill in the blanks to solve the puzzle below:

     M __ __   The most complex mammal.

     A __ __ __ __ __   Mammals belong to this kingdom.

     M __ __ __ __ __ __ __ __ __   Mammals who carry their young in a pouch.

     M __ __ __ __ __ __   A gland that makes milk for newborns.

     A __ __   _____ mammals are warm-blooded.

     L __ __ __   __ __ __ __ __ __ __ __

                           Most mammals give birth to _____ _____.

II.   Choose the best answer to complete the following sentences.

1.   _____ show us that mammals are the _____ animals.

2.   Mammal mothers _____ their young by feeding them _____.

3.   The spine is made up of small bones called _____.

4.   Whales are _____ since they can maintain a constant body temperature.

5.   Pigs are mammals so they must have _____ on their bodies.

6.   Mammals have skulls with large _____.

7.   Some scientists believe _____ are the ancestors of modern mammals.

8.   Mammals have become the most _____ group of animals.

9.   A mammal can digest food quickly because of its _____ teeth.

10. List five main characteristics of mammals.

    A. _____

    B. _____

    C. _____

    D. _____

    E. _____

Analyze: Why do you think mammals survived when the dinosaurs died?

_____

_____

_____

_____

Keeping Track: *Classification of Mammals*

Mammals, like all living things, are placed into groups, which makes it easier to study and learn about them. For example, suppose you wanted to go to the store and look for a certain CD you've been wanting. To make it easier for you to find the CD you want, the store organizes them according to the type of music, and then in alphabetical order. In the same way, all **organisms** (living things) are organized or put into groups based on the traits they have in common. Scientists look at organisms' similarities as well as their differences, which helps them to place the organisms into their proper groups. They are grouped and regrouped until every organism in the group is one of a kind. Then the group has only one species in it, and each species is given a scientific name. The name given to the organism is based on the Latin language, because Latin is the common scientific language throughout the world. In this way, scientists can keep track of the many different kinds of organisms.

Carolus Linnaeus developed a system of assigning every organism a name and of classifying each organism according to its system, size, shape, color, and method of obtaining food. This two-word naming system is called **binomial nomenclature** and was developed to help scientists avoid errors in communication. Binomial means "two names." The two-word species name is commonly called the organism's **scientific name**, and it is always written in italics. The scientific name is made up of the **genus** name and the **species** name. The first letter of the first word (genus name) is always capitalized, and the second word (species name) is always in lower case. An example of a scientific name is *Canis familiaris* (the dog). A specific name for every organism avoids confusion when scientists communicate because there are often too many common names for an animal, which can be misleading. For example, prairie dogs are more similar to squirrels than dogs; a starfish is not a fish, yet a seahorse is a fish.

The modern classification used today is based on a five-kingdom system. These kingdoms are *Animal, Plant, Fungi, Protista,* and *Monera.* The science of classifying and naming organisms is called **taxonomy**. To be considered an animal, the organism must have **eukaryotic cells** (cells with a nucleus), it must have many cells, and it must be able to move about. It is not able to make its own food but must eat other organisms and digest its food.

Mammals are classified or divided into three main subclasses, according to how their young develop. The first are the **monotremes**, which lay eggs with leathery shells and incubate them. The hatchlings lick milk from the mother's skin. The duck-billed platypus is the most common monotreme. A second division is a group called **marsupials**, the pouched mammals. Pouched mammals give birth to immature offspring, which must crawl into the mother's pouch to feed and finish developing. The best known marsupial is the kangaroo. When a kangaroo is first born, it is the size of a honeybee. It has no fur and cannot see. Once developed, the little joey (a young kangaroo) crawls out of the pouch. The **placental mammals** make up the third group and largest; most mammals fall into this group. The embryo remains inside the female mammal until it is fully formed. This development time is called **gestation**. Gestation periods range from 16 days in hamsters to 650 days in elephants. The embryo develops in a saclike organ called a **placenta**. The embryo obtains food and oxygen from the mother, and its waste is removed through an umbilical cord. The **umbilical cord** attaches the embryo (the developing offspring) to the placenta, forming a connecting link between the mother and her embryo. These three divisions of mammals are just the beginning; mammals are then divided into 18 smaller groups, or **orders**.

Name:_____ Date: _____

Keeping Track: *Classification of Mammals Activity*

Monotreme (egg-laying mammal)   Marsupial (pouched mammal)

Placental Mammal (developing embryo)

1.   Identify and explain the three ways mammals are classified.

a. _____

_____

_____

b. _____

_____

_____

c. _____

_____

_____

Name:_____ Date:_____

Keeping Track: *Classification Review*

To the student observer: Classification puts things in their correct place. By drawing conclusions from the lesson, answer the questions below.

1. What does it mean to classify things? _____

   _____

2. Why do scientists classify living things? _____

   _____

3. Explain binomial nomenclature. _____

   _____

   _____

4. Who developed binomial nomenclature? _____

5. How do you write an organism's scientific name? _____

   _____

6. On what language is the classification system based? _____

7. What is the science of classifying or naming organisms called? _____

8. List the five kingdoms modern classification is based on.

   _____   _____   _____

   _____   _____

Analyze: Explain how you use classification in your daily life.

_____

_____

_____

_____

Name:_____ Date:_____

Using a Dichotomous Key: *Student Activity*

To the student observer: Taxonomists are scientists who classify. They have developed many keys that aid in the identification of organisms that may be unknown to you. Let's see if you can use a dichotomous key successfully. Good luck, observers!

A **dichotomous key** contains detailed lists of traits to help scientists classify organisms. Dichotomous keys are arranged in steps with two descriptive statements at each step. To use a key, you must always start with the first pair of descriptions. The descriptions are usually labeled as 1a and 1b, 2a and 2b, 3a and 3b, and so on. Start with description 1; from there you will see either a name of a species or directions to go on to the next set of descriptions. If you can follow the directions in the key, you have the recipe for success in finding the correct name for your species.

Problem: Can you follow the key to identify large native cats in the United States?

Materials:

Paper and pencil (A pencil makes it easier to change your mind.)
Optional: Colored pencils to color the cats below

Procedure:

1. Study the cats below and compare them to the pictures of the cats your teacher has.
2. Begin with the first pair of descriptions in the key to identify the species of Cat A.
3. Write the common and scientific name for Cat A.
4. Repeat the process to identify the species of Cat B.
5. Write the common and scientific name for Cat B.

Cat A

Cat B

Common name: _____   **Common name:** _____

Scientific name: **Scientific name:**

_____ _____   _____ _____

* **Teacher note:** Obtain a color picture of Cat A and Cat B for students to observe during the lesson.

Name:_____ Date:_____

Using a Dichotomous Key: *Student Activity (cont.)*

Key to Native Cats of North America

1a. If the cat has a short tail .... go to step 2
1b. If the cat has a long tail .... go to step 3

2a. If the cat has long ear tufts tipped with black and no cheek ruff .... *Lynx lynx* / lynx
2b. If the cat has indistinct spots, short ear tufts, and cheek ruff .... *Lynx rufus* / bobcat

3a. If the cat has a plainly-colored body .... go to step 4
3b. If the cat has a patterned body .... go to step 5

4a. If the cat is yellowish with white below .... *Puma concolor* / mountain lion
4b. If the cat is brown or black all over .... *Herpailurus yagouaroundi* / jaguarundi

5a. If the cat has a patterned body with tan and black .... go to step 6
5b. If the cat has black-bordered brown spots in lines .... *Leopardus pardalis* / ocelot

6a. If the cat is large, spotted with black rings in rows .... *Panthera onca* / jaguar
6b. If the cat is small, with irregularly-shaped spots with four stripes on back and one on the neck .... *Felis wiedii* / margay

Analyze:

1. According to the key, how many species of native cats live in North America? _____

2. What was the first trait used to name the cats? _____

3. What characteristics would scientists look at next? _____

_____

Conclusion: Explain why it wouldn't be a good idea for you to begin in the middle of this key.

_____

_____

_____

_____

* **Teacher Note:** You might want to extend the activity or offer extra credit by identifying the bobcat, jaguarundi, and jaguar. These three cats are also represented in the key. However, prior to the lesson, you should find a colored picture of each cat to display for students' use.

Name:_____ Date:_____

What's the Name?: *Scientific Names*

To the student observer: Scientific names are used to avoid mistakes in communication. There are more than 4,500 species of mammals. Look at the list of mammals below. Using reference materials, give the scientific name for each mammal. After you have named each mammal, make an analysis from your list and answer the questions below.

1. Coyote _____

2. Dog _____

3. Fox (red) _____

4. House cat _____

5. Lion _____

6. Puma _____

7. Tiger _____

8. Wolf (gray) _____

Analyze: What observation can you make about your research above?

_____

_____

_____

_____

_____

Conclusion: Based on the information you collected from your research, what do you think the genus name must be for the dingo? (The dingo is a wild dog in Australia.)

_____

* **Teacher note:** Provide reference materials in advance or take the students to the reference area to do research. This could be a computer lab assignment if you have one available to your students.

9

Name:_____ Date:_____

How Are Organisms Named?: *Observer Journal Activities*

ACTIVITY 1

To the student observer: Can you give a scientific name to a new organism? Think about the process involved and what you've learned about mammals.

Procedure:

1. Draw a fictitious mammal in your journal.

2. Give your mammal a scientific name.

3. Make sure your name is Latinized and infers information about the species.

Analysis:

1. Present your new mammal to the class. Ask them to guess a name.

2. Why do scientists use Latin in giving organisms their names?

ACTIVITY 2

To the student observer: Can you make a report in a science journal?

Procedure:

1. Select a field guide for mammals from your resource area. Most field guides use descriptions that lead to the identification of the animal.

2. Describe the parts of the field guide.

3. Select two mammals that, in your opinion, closely resemble each other. Compare and contrast them.

4. Use labeled diagrams if you find them helpful.

* **Teacher note:** You will need to locate a Latin dictionary for Activity 1. Stress the importance of recording information in a journal. All budding scientists need to be observant and keep good records.

Mammal Orders

To the student observer: A **mammologist** is a person who studies mammals. Most mammalogists agree that all the known living species of mammals fall into one of 18 major orders. Mammals are grouped according to structural similarities and fossil evidence. You will soon see that this arrangement reveals some unexpected relationships. Surprisingly, some scientists believe man is more closely related to the shrew than any other order. However, man has been placed in the primate group. Let's examine how scientists have organized the mammals.

Marsupials—Pouched Mammals

The marsupials have been divided into seven different groups. Most of the 250 living species of marsupials live in Australia or on nearby islands. The only marsupial that lives in the United States is the opossum. A **marsupial** is a mammal that gives birth to tiny immature offspring that must finish developing inside the **marsupium**, or pouch, which gives the group its name. The amount of time an offspring must stay in its mother's pouch varies, depending on the species.

The young of the American opossum are born undeveloped and blind, yet they have claws and are strong enough to crawl into their mother's pouch. After they leave their mother's pouch, the babies spend several weeks riding on their mother's back, clinging to her fur. They have five toes and an opposable inside toe on their hind legs. This allows them to hold on to things and helps them climb. The opossum is a **nocturnal** animal (it is active at night) and is interested in eating almost anything. When attacked, the opossum will pretend to be dead. Have you ever heard the expression "playing 'possum"?

Mammal Orders

Monotremes—Egg-laying Mammals

It's not easy to have one statement that applies to every kind of animal. Although we say mammals give birth to live young, there are two who do not. They both live in Australia; one is the platypus, and the other is the echidna. Both of these mammals lay eggs. Because they both are egg-laying mammals, they belong to the order *monotremata*. No monotremes live in the United States.

The duck-billed platypus lives in a burrow. It has a flattened tail, fur, short legs, and a muzzle that looks like a duck's bill. Its flat, beaver-like tail and webbed feet are adaptations to an aquatic lifestyle. It spends most of its time in the water eating worms and crayfish. When on land, it folds the webbing on its feet back and uses its claws to dig a burrow. A female platypus digs a long tunnel when she is ready to lay her eggs. She prepares the nest and protects her eggs by curling her body around them. When the babies hatch, they lap milk from slits on her belly. At about four months old, they leave the nest.

There are two species of echidna—the long-nosed echidna and the short-nosed echidna, also known as the spiny anteater. Both have long spines, heavy claws, and sensitive snouts, which are used to search for food. The short-nosed echidna looks for insects, while the long-nosed echidna eats mostly earthworms. The female echidna carries a single leathery egg in a pouch that forms on her belly at the beginning of the breeding season. After about ten days, the

egg hatches. The blind and hairless baby, no bigger than a raisin, sucks milk from glands that are inside the pouch. The off-spring grows quickly. After several weeks, sharp spines develop. Then it can no longer remain in its mother's pouch. After several years, the young echidna is fully grown.

The Placental Mammals—Lions and tigers and bears—Oh my!

Ninety-five percent of all the mammals are **placental mammals**. They are very diversified. These mammals make their homes in water, on land, and in the air. They all have special adaptations for movement and obtaining food that fit the environment in which they live.

Land Mammals: Rodentia—Gnawing mammals

The largest order of mammals is *Rodentia*. There are more than 1,700 species of rodents. Beavers, chipmunks, mice, and squirrels are all rodents. Rodents are herbivores and are called gnawing animals because they have a pair of long, sharp teeth in each jaw. These long teeth continue to grow and give them their buck-toothed look. Their name comes from the Latin verb *rodere*, which means "to gnaw." They are mostly small animals with a high rate of reproduction. The largest rodent is the capybara, an overgrown guinea pig from South America. It may reach a length of over three feet. The largest rodent in the United States is the beaver.

Mammal Orders

Insectivora—Insect-eaters

The name *Insectivora* comes from the Latin language and means "insect-eater." However, this doesn't mean they all eat insects. The smallest mammals fall into this group. The tiny shrew, mole, and hedgehog are examples of insectivores. The reason these animals were grouped together by scientists is because their teeth are so much alike. Each has many small teeth and a special check tooth with points called **cusps**. The cusps, as well as the insect-eater's long skull and narrow snout, are useful for eating and finding insects. They spend all their time in search of food.

Insectivora–Shrew

Lagomorpha—The hopping mammals

Pikas along with rabbits and hares are the only two families in the order *Lagomorpha*. Rabbits and hares have long ears, long and powerful hind legs, clawed toes, and stubby tails. Pikas have rounded ears, legs of equal length, no noticeable tails, and are smaller in size. Although similar to rodents, lagomorphs (lay-go-MORFS) differ in the structure of their teeth. They have two pairs of upper incisors. A lagomorph's diet consists of leaves, grasses, and bark.

Lagomorpha–Pika

Mammal Orders

Ugulates: Hoofed Mammals

Artiodactyla—The even-toed

Most of the members of the group *Artiodactyla* are medium to large in size. They are herbivores with large, flat molars and a complex digestive system. They have an even number of toes. Pigs, cows, hippopotamuses, camels, sheep, and giraffes make up this order. This order also contains the animals that have antlers that are shed at certain times of the year, which include deer, moose, elk, and caribou.

Perissodactyla—The odd-toed

Like the artiodactyles, the members of the order *Perissodactyla* are medium- to large-sized animals. They are herbivores with flat teeth for grinding plant material. Both groups consist of grazing animals; however, the perissodactyles have an odd number of toes. The horse has only one visible toe, and the rhinoceros has three toes. The perissodactyles that live in the United States include the horse, the donkey, and the mule. The zebra and tapirs are also members of this order.

Proboscidea—The trunk-nosed

The order *Proboscidea* has only two species: Indian elephants and African elephants. They have elongated noses that form a trunk and a pair of enlarged incisors that forms tusks. Their skin is very leathery. They are massive animals with a large head, flat ears, a short neck, and very little hair. They are herbivores who graze for as many as 18 hours a day.

Mammal Orders

Carnivores—Meat-eaters

The most common families in this order include the dogs, bears, raccoons, pandas, hyenas, and cats. Most of the 240 species of the order *Carnivora* are strictly meat-eating mammals, but there are many exceptions that eat berries, nuts, and bamboo shoots. Carnivores have a pair of long sharp teeth (canines), strong jaws, and clawed toes. They are considered the strongest and most intelligent group of mammals.

Pinnipedia—Aquatic Carnivores

The order *Carnivora* includes a suborder of animals adapted to aquatic life called the *Pinnipedia*. The word means "having winged feet," which refers to the animals' finlike feet or flippers. The pinnipeds include the walruses, sea lions, and seals. Pinnipeds have limbs for swimming, a streamlined body, and a thick layer of fat for insulation from the icy waters. These carnivores return to land to reproduce.

Primates—Opposable thumbs

There are about 175 species of primates. They live in trees or on the ground. They are divided into two main groups: the **prosimians** or primitive primates and the more advanced **anthropoids**. This order contains the widest range of development, from the smallest and least intelligent to the highest form of animal life. Primates consist of tree shrews, lemurs, monkeys, apes, and man. Primates have long arms with grasping hands and opposable thumbs. They have nails rather than claws. They have eyes that face forward and large, complex brains. Primates are omnivores and will eat whatever is available. They are very social animals that live in family units called **troupes**. With the exception of humans, most primates live in the tropical and subtropical parts of the world. As the most advanced animals to inhabit the earth, we, as humans, must take our responsibility seriously—we are the caretakers of the planet.

Mammal Orders

Cetaceans—Marine Mammals

The order *Cetacea* (suh-TAY-shuh) includes dolphins, porpoises, and whales. Cetaceans have torpedo-shaped bodies with a long, pointed head and no neck. They have forelimbs that are modified into flippers for swimming and have a horizontal tail; otherwise, they resemble a fish. As mammals, cetaceans do not have gills and must come to the surface for air. They breathe through blowholes on the tops of their heads. All of the cetaceans in the United States are marine or saltwater mammals, and this group includes the largest of the mammals. They are the only mammals that are strictly aquatic; they spend their entire lives in the water. Cetaceans reproduce in water and usually have only one offspring at a time.

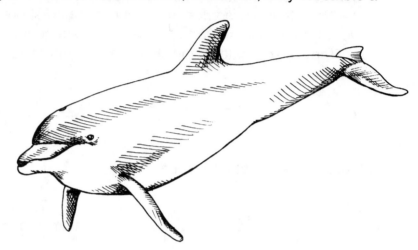

Sirenians

The order *Sirenia* (sy-REEN-ee-uh) is a small group of aquatic mammals that includes the manatees and the dugongs. Sirenians have a barrel-shaped body with flipper-like forelimbs, no hind limbs, and a flat horizontal tail. They feed on aquatic vegetation.

Mammal Orders

Chiroptera—Bats, the Flying Mammals

The order *Chiroptera* (ki-ROP-ter-uh) is the second-largest order of mammals. All of the 925 species of chiropterans are commonly known as bats. Bats are small **nocturnal** (active at night) animals that can fly. They are the only mammals that actually fly, rather than glide. The four elongated fingers of each hand support the flight membrane, which is also attached to the ankles and sometimes the tail. Powerful muscles move the wings and help the bat fly up to 65 kilometers per hour. Bats live wherever the climate is warm enough to support trees. Bats migrate to warmer climates in the winter. The smallest bat weighs only four grams, while the largest bat weighs as much as 1.5 kilograms.

Bats have a diversified diet, which is why they have such a variety of teeth. Insect-eating bats have curved teeth that mash the insects into a paste. Bats that eat fruit have teeth that are flattened so they can grind the plants. Vampire bats have razor-sharp teeth. These bats feed on large mammals by cutting their skin and lapping up the blood. Vampire bats do not suck the blood out of their prey's body.

Bats have small eyes, which give them poor vision; however, they are not blind. The expression, "blind as a bat," makes it sound as though they can't see. Having small eyes is not a disadvantage; bats find their way around perfectly by using **echolocation**. When the bat hunts, it emits a high-pitched squeak that we can't hear. When these sounds strike a solid object, they bounce back as echoes. The bat's ears pick up these echoes and form a mental picture of its surroundings. It can tell if the echoes come from an insect or something solid in its path. Fruit-eating bats do not use echolocation to find their food, because fruit is stationary. Bats can be social animals, and millions may roost together. Other species are solitary and prefer to roost alone in trees or under the eaves of buildings.

Bats are beneficial and should be protected. They eat insect pests such as mosquitoes. However, they can carry diseases such as rabies.

Name:_____ Date: _____

Mammalian Orders: *Comprehension*

To the student observer: Why are humans considered animals? _____
_____
_____

Directions: By drawing conclusions from the lesson, answer the questions below.

1. What are adaptations? _____
   _____

2. Who are mammalogists? _____
   _____

3. What characteristic must a mammal have to be called a marsupial? _____
   _____

4. What two exceptions exist in the class *mammalia*? _____
   _____

5. What is the largest order of mammals? _____

6. What is the largest rodent in the United States? _____

7. Why do rabbits and hares have long ears and long hind legs? _____
   _____

8. Name two mammals that shed their antlers at certain times of the year.
   _____

9. Which order includes the highest form of animal life? _____
   _____

10. What are the two orders of marine mammals, and where do they live? ____
    _____

11. Identify the only mammal that can fly. _____

12. What is *echolocation*? _____
    _____

13. Which group includes the seals and walruses? _____

Name:_____ Date:_____

Problem-Solving: *Echolocation*

Flying Acrobats

Bats are the only mammals that truly fly. They are able to fly about in the night with the greatest of ease. Have you ever wondered how they do this? If you recall from the lesson, they emit an extremely high-pitched sound through their mouths or their noses. The sound is so high in pitch that humans cannot hear the sounds. Bats also make sounds a human can hear, such as whining sounds or even loud squeaks. Amazingly, in complete darkness, they are able to hunt for fast-flying insects, while at the same time avoid branches and wires. They use the sound waves they send out to help guide them by a process called **echolocation**. The sounds they send out travel in front of them and bounce back to their ears, telling them if the object is prey or if it is a solid object and needs to be avoided.

Directions: By drawing conclusions from the lesson, answer the questions below.

1. What happens to a sound wave when it comes in contact with an object that is solid?

_____

_____

2. How does echolocation help bats locate things in the dark? _____

_____

_____

3. Bats have very large ears. How are the large ears an adaptation for hearing?

_____

_____

Analyze: Explain what you think would happen if a bat were placed in a soundproof room and allowed to hunt for food.

_____

_____

_____

_____

Name:_____ Date: _____

Different Kinds of Mammals: *Adaptation Activity*

To the student observer: Mammals are very adaptable and are found in all types of habitats. Monotremes make up one order of mammals. The marsupials have been divided into seven orders. The placental mammals make up the other orders. Each order has adaptations that help identify it. **Adaptations** are traits that help the mammal survive in its environment.

Below is a list of the common orders and the characteristics of those orders. See if you can give an example for each order, based on the characteristics.

Order	Characteristics	Example
1. Monotremata	Egg-laying mammals	
2. Marsupials	Pouched mammals	
3. Insectivora	Insect-eaters; long skulls; narrow snouts; clawed feet; the smallest mammals	
4. Chiroptera	Front limbs for flying; active at night; eat fruits, insects, or blood; use echolocation	
5. Rodentia	Gnawing animals with chisel-like teeth	
6. Lagomorpha	Have long hind legs for jumping and running; have two pairs of upper incisors	
7. Carnivora	Long, sharp canine teeth; five toes on the front feet; eat meat mostly, but some eat vegetation	
8. Artiodactyla	Even-toed hooves; herbivores; some with antlers; are medium to large in size	
9. Perissodactyla	Odd-toed hooves; herbivores; long jaws with flattened teeth for grinding vegetation	
10. Proboscidea	Elongated nose; a trunk; enlarged incisors for tusks; leathery skin	
11. Primates	Long arms; grasping hands; opposable thumbs; eyes face forward; are omnivores	
12. Cetacea	Forelimbs like flippers; they breath through blowholes; are strictly aquatic	
13. Sirenia	Aquatic; large in size; broad head; flattened tail; feed on vegetation	

* **Teacher note:** If you have strong students, you may want to use this as an introduction for the mammal orders. (It is suggested that you use the word bank from the optional word bank page.)

20

Smile—*Let's See Those Mammal Teeth!*

Almost all mammals have teeth modified for the food they eat. These teeth perform special jobs for the mammal, depending on how the mammal obtains its food and what it eats. Scientists can tell what kind of food a mammal eats by examining its teeth. After this lesson, you'll be able to tell what kind of food a mammal eats and to which group the mammal is classified, according to its food intake.

Food is the fuel that makes the body machine work. Without food, living things would quickly lose energy and die. Mammals live in a variety of habitats and eat a variety of foods. The mammal must first find the food that meets its bodily needs and then actually get the food to its mouth. This might sound simple to you, but many problems arise. A giraffe with its long neck doesn't do well when bending its legs to reach vegetation on the ground. A short-necked grazing animal, like the cow, wouldn't do well if it was suddenly transported to a forest environment. The canopy above would prevent the growth of grass, and its short neck wouldn't let it reach the foliage on the trees. With meat-eaters the problem is actually greater. They must be able to find suitable prey and then capture it. They have to run it down, ambush it, or use some hunting technique to be able to get their food. This is only the beginning; the food must meet the body's needs by supplying the nourishment needed for survival.

The mouth itself must be equipped with the necessary machinery to deal with the food it receives. In most mammals, this machinery is the type of teeth the animal has. Most mammals have four different kinds of teeth: incisors, canines, premolars, and molars. **Incisors**, at the front of the jaws, are for nipping, cutting, or gnawing. The **canines**, which are next to the incisors, are for seizing and tearing. The **premolars** and **molars** lie in the back of the jaw and are for grinding and chewing. All of these teeth are modified to fit the needs of the animal and to aid in its survival. Sometimes the modification goes so far that the teeth are no longer used for eating purposes. The tusks of the elephant are an example of extreme modification. The tusks are no longer used for eating; they are used for rooting for food, for attack, and for defense.

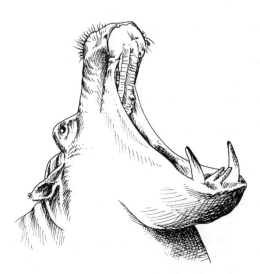

Mammals may be classified into three basic groups according to their food intake. **Herbivores**, strictly vegetarians, make up one group. The **carnivores**, or meat-eaters, make up a second group. **Omnivores**, which eat both plants and animals, make up the third group. Mammals, like all animals, eat in order to obtain the energy needed to carry out life activities. The energy originates from the sun and is transferred to the animals through food. A food chain or food web can model this transfer of energy. Producers make up the first link in any food chain. **Producers** (plants) capture the energy from the sun. The second link of a food chain is usually an herbivore, an organism that feeds only on producers. The third link of a food chain is a carnivore, an animal that feeds on other animals. The fourth link is a top carnivore, which feeds on other carnivores.

Name:_____ Date:_____

Smile—*Let's See Those Mammal Teeth!*

To the student observer: How many different kinds of teeth do you have? _____

Except for a few special cases, mammals generally eat their food in one of three ways—by gnawing, by grinding, or by tearing—and their teeth have become adapted accordingly.

Directions: By drawing conclusions from the lesson, answer the questions below.

1. What kind of teeth do most mammals have? _____

_____

2. Why are the canine teeth in wolves sharper than the canine teeth of deer?

_____

_____

3. Why do beavers and other rodents have sharper incisors than a cow?

_____

_____

4. Which teeth are located in front? _____

5. What animal has gone through extreme modification and no longer uses its canines for chewing?

_____

6. List and define the three ways mammals are classified according to their food intake.

   a. _____

   _____

   b. _____

   _____

   c. _____

   _____

Analyze: How do your teeth relate to your diet? _____

_____

Name:_____ Date:_____

Mammal Teeth Activity

To the student observer: Study the drawings below and use your knowledge to label the teeth: **Canines, Incisors, Molars, and Premolars**

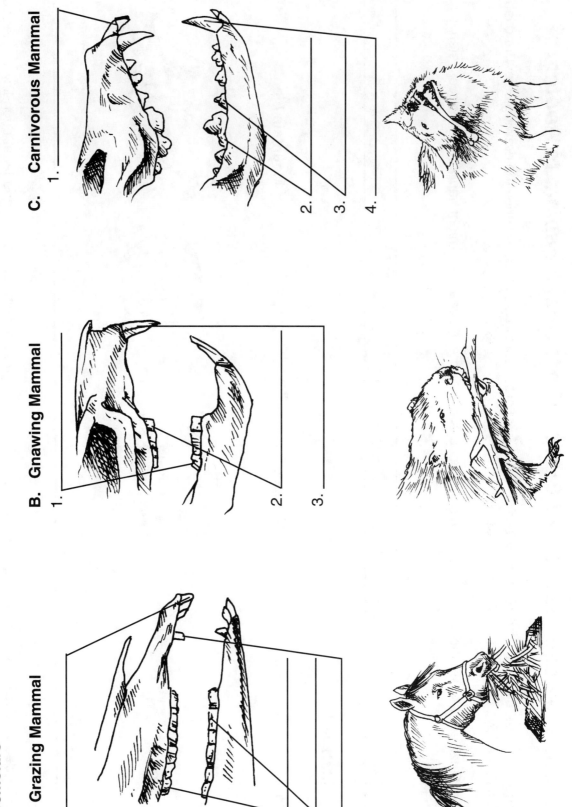

A. Grazing Mammal

1.

2.

3.

4.

B. Gnawing Mammal

1.

2.

3.

C. Carnivorous Mammal

1.

2.

3.

4.

Name:_____ Date:_____

Food Chain Model: *Transfer of Energy From One Organism to Another*

To the student observer: In any community, energy flows from producers to consumers. Study the drawing below, and label each link in the food chain.

Analyze: Grizzly bears are the top carnivores in some ecosystems. What do you think might happen in that ecosystem if the number of grizzly bears suddenly declined?

I. **FOOD CHAIN**

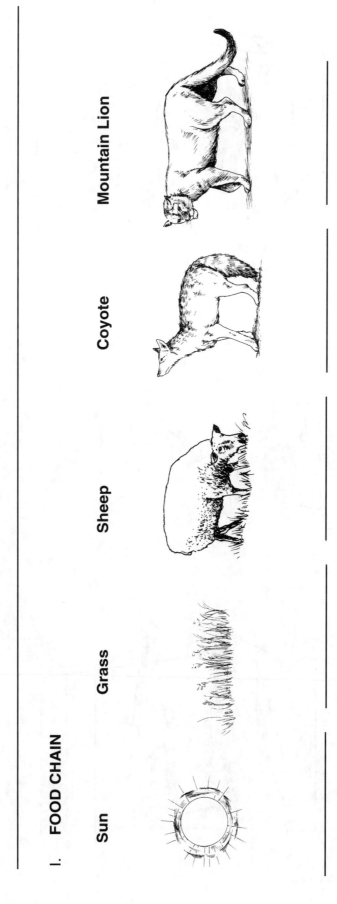

Sun   Grass   Sheep   Coyote   Mountain Lion

II. **Extended Activity:** Following your teacher's directions, design your own food chain and label each link in the food chain on your own paper.

* **Teacher note:** You might want to provide the optional word bank from the word bank page.

Name: _____ Date: _____

Making Observations Activity

To the Student Observer: How observant are you? Use your powers of observation to do the following activity.

Procedure: Choose a pet or animal from your neighborhood that you know well, and observe it. Make sure it is a mammal. A dog, cat, horse, gerbil, or hamster will do for this activity. If you live in a rural setting, you might choose a cow, pig, fox, sheep, squirrel, or deer for your project. Observe the mammal in its natural setting for several days. Use an encyclopedia or the Internet to add additional information to your observations. Complete the table below with your observations and the information you gained by reading about this mammal.

Observations of a _____ (Mammal)

Recorded Data and Observations	
Characteristics	**Observation/Information**
Scientific Classification Kingdom, phyla, class, order, family	
Outer Covering	
Teeth	
Food	
Reproduction (Type) Placental, Marsupial, Monotreme	
Gestation Period (length of embryo development)	
Other Characteristics	

Conclusions:

1. Upon observing the mammal's teeth and food choices, can you classify it by the food it eats and the type of teeth it has as an omnivore, herbivore, or a carnivore?

    _____

2. On your own paper, explain how the mammal is suited to its environment based on the characteristics you observed.

The Way You Do the Things You Do: *Mammal Behavior*

Mammals, like all animals, react to changes in their environments. The way an organism acts is called **behavior**. The reaction of the mammal is called a **response**. A mammal's response to some change in its environment demonstrates a particular behavior. The something in the environment that the mammal responds to is called a **stimulus**. The stimulus is the cause of the behavior. Heat, pressure, chemicals, sound, light, and even gravity are examples of stimuli. When mammals interact with the environment or one another, they are demonstrating some type of behavior.

Most behaviors are focused on survival. Behaviors help mammals avoid predators and find food, water, shelter, and mates. Behaviors fall into two categories. **Innate** behaviors are present at birth and are found in all members of the same species. Behavior that is acquired as a result of experience is **learned** behavior.

An innate behavior such as a newborn mammal nursing doesn't require thinking. It is an automatic response in which the brain is not involved. In mammals, behaviors involved in mating, caring for young, communicating, migrating, and finding food are innate behaviors. There are two types of innate behaviors, reflex and instinct. A **reflex** is an automatic response the mammal cannot control. The ability of a cat to land on its feet from a fall is an example of reflex. Blinking, yawning, sneezing, shivering, and increased heart rate are all reflexes. **Instincts** are a bit more complex. The brain is involved, but it is not a learned activity. Beavers building a dam or bears hibernating during the winter are examples of instinctive behaviors. A mammal migrating in response to temperature is also an example of instinct.

Learned behaviors include conditioning, trial-and-error, reasoning, and imprinting. **Conditioning** is a behavior that is a response to stimuli that wouldn't normally cause that behavior. Ivan Pavlov's experiment is an example of conditioning. Pavlov trained a dog to salivate at the sound of a bell. Each time he fed the dog, he would ring a bell. The dog soon associated food with the sound of the bell. **Trial-and-error learning** would be like a hungry mouse learning how to run a maze to find the reward at the end. In the wild, a mouse shuffling about in the grass finds a berry underneath. The berry is the reward that reinforces the behavior. If it happens often enough, the mouse will eventually learn to turn leaves over in search of food. **Reasoning** is thinking of a solution to a problem by using past experiences to help solve the new prob-

lem. Insight is required to interpret the new situation and relate it to a memory of a past experience. In an experiment, a chimpanzee was placed in a room with several boxes. Bananas were placed high above its head. After a period of time in which the chimpanzee appeared to be thinking things over, the chimpanzee stacked the boxes, climbed up, and reached the bananas! Goslings demonstrate **imprinting** when newly-hatched goslings learn to follow the first thing they see, thinking it is their mother. Once imprinting has taken place, it is permanent. This type of learning is a way for offspring to establish a bond with their parents.

The Way You Do the Things You Do: *Mammal Behavior (cont.)*

Mammals use sounds, facial expressions, visual displays, and scents or **pheromones** (fayr-oh-mohnz) to convey information. They have courtship behaviors to attract mates and territorial behaviors that keep unwanted guests away. They mark their territories to claim living space, food, and mates for themselves. Sometimes they fight to the death to have a place to call their own.

Mammals also interact with their environment and respond to periodic cycles and rhythms. Seasonal changes, such as migration and hibernation, and daily activities, such as being active at night (**nocturnal**) or active by day (**diurnal**), fall into this category. I guess you could say they move with rhythm. Mammals seem to know when it is time to make these cyclic journeys from one region to another and back again. An internal timer, or biological clock, maintains the body's natural cycles and rhythms. If the rhythm repeats every 24 hours, it is called a **circadian rhythm**. The pattern of human sleep is an example of circadian rhythm.

Name:_____ Date:_____

Mammal Behavior Reinforcement

To the student observer: Do you think the behaviors of mammals such as dolphins and elephants should be modified when they are trained to perform at theme parks or zoos? (Support your answer.)

_____

_____

_____

Completion: Write the word or term that best completes each statement.

1. Marking a territory with pheromones is an example of _____ _____.

2. _____ behavior is present at birth and does not require experience.

3. A pattern that repeats every 24 hours is called a _____ _____.

4. A _____ is the way a mammal reacts to changes in its environment.

5. Mammals' reactions are responses to _____.

6. A _____ allows a mammal to respond quickly without conscious thought.

7. When _____, humans apply memories of past experiences to solve new problems.

8. _____ develops a special bond between offspring and parents shortly after birth and is permanent.

Directions: By drawing conclusions from the lesson, answer the questions below.

1. What are the two categories of behavior? _____

_____

2. What are the two types of innate behaviors? _____

_____

3. What are the four learned behaviors? _____

_____

4. What do mammals use to convey information or communicate? _____

_____

Endangered and Threatened: *Animals We Must Protect*

To the student observer: Do you know who is counting on you for their protection?

Endangered animals are those in need of protection in order to survive. They are in immediate danger of becoming **extinct** (no longer living). The animals that are already extinct are animals we will never see again. There are over 5,000 animal species around the globe that have been classified as endangered, and many thousands more become extinct each year before biologists can identify them. The primary causes of species extinction or endangerment are habitat destruction, commercial exploitation (hunting and selling of animal parts), and pollution. Habitat destruction is the factor that threatens survival the most. The world's habitats are changing faster than most species can adapt to them. The destruction of ecosystems, such as forests, coral reefs, or wetlands, leads to the loss of organisms that live in these areas. We depend on species diversity (variety of plants and animals) to provide us with food, clean air and water, and fertile soil. There are two degrees of endangerment. **Endangered species** are in immediate risk of extinction and probably cannot survive without human intervention. **Threatened species** are abundant in parts of their range but are declining in total numbers and are at risk in the future.

Animals are hunted for many reasons. Some are hunted for food; some are hunted for products that can be made from them; many are hunted for their fur, skin, tusks, or horns. Some are captured and sold to zoos and animal shows. Some are killed because they are considered dangerous. Even though many endangered animals are protected by law or special refuges, many are still being killed by **poachers** (someone who hunts illegally). Poachers are willing to break the laws because they know they can sell what they kill for a lot of money.

The human population on the earth has had the biggest effect on animals. More people mean more farms to raise food, more houses to be built, and more roads for transportation. Land is being cleared, forests are cut down, and bogs and swamps are drained. Every time this happens, some animal's habitat is changed, and it has to adapt or face the possibility of extinction. The more people there are, the more pollution is created. The overuse of insecticides has lead to the decline of many birds and the end of many fish. Laws are trying to change this, but pollution is still a major problem.

Reasons Animals Become Endangered

Habitat Loss	Unregulated or Illegal Hunting	Pesticides/Pollution
Predators	Disease	

Some Endangered Mammals

Mountain Gorilla	African Elephant	Snow Leopard	Sperm Whale
Jaguar	Bandicoot	Tiger	Black Rhinoceros
Giant Panda	Pygmy Hippopotamus	Florida Manatee	Ocelot
Lemur	Bighorn Sheep	Blue Whale	Gray Wolf
Bobcat	Indiana Bat	Gazelle	Silvery Gibbon
Red Wolf	Black-Footed Ferret	Wolverine	Red Kangaroo

29

Name:_____ Date: _____

Endangered and Threatened: *Reinforcement*

To the student observer: Let's see what you have learned about endangered mammals.

A fact is a statement that can be verified as true.
   Fact: Endangered animals are those in danger of becoming extinct.

An opinion is a statement that cannot be verified as true.
   Opinion: Endangered animals are all dangerous animals.

Write "F" for fact or "O" for opinion on the line by each statement.

_____ 1. Animals should never be killed.

_____ 2. Pollution of air and water has caused many animals to become endangered.

_____ 3. The lemur is an endangered animal.

_____ 4. The zoo is the best place for endangered animals.

_____ 5. People's needs are more important than animals.

_____ 6. Poaching is an illegal activity.

_____ 7. One reason the giant panda is endangered is that it reproduces at a slow rate.

_____ 8. Killing an animal is okay if you are going to eat it.

By drawing conclusions from the lesson, answer the questions below.

1. What is the difference between an endangered animal and one that is threatened?

   _____

   _____

2. Why are animals becoming endangered? _____

   _____

   _____

3. What is the primary cause of endangerment? _____

   _____

   _____

Analyze: How do you feel about endangered animals? Why do people still hunt endangered animals?

_____

_____

Name: _____ Date: _____

Endangered Mammals: *Research and Writing Project*

To the student observer: Issue an invitation to an endangered mammal to join you for dinner.

Analyze: If you could invite an endangered mammal to join you for dinner tonight, which one would you ask?

Dr. Elizabeth N. Danejerd, field biologist for the Fish and Wildlife Service, was out in the field tagging endangered lemurs. She began to think about the animals that once lived there but no longer exist. She wondered: If she could invite an endangered animal to dinner, which one would she invite? She decided to invite a lemur to dinner to learn how the species had become endangered. She soon found herself making a list of interview questions to ask her guest.

Teacher directions: As a class, research endangered animals and brainstorm to add to the list of endangered mammals below. From the class list, have each student choose an endangered mammal that interests him or her. Instruct each student to invite the mammal to join him or her for dinner to share its story. Have each student make a list of interview questions for his or her chosen mammal and then do research to find the answers to the questions. He or she should then write the answers in the form of a magazine or newspaper article on a separate sheet of paper. If time allows, have students share their stories with the class.

Alternative assignment: If you have access to a computer lab, the students could make brochures to inform people about each mammal's need for protection.

Sample list of endangered animals:

Mountain Gorilla	African Elephant	Snow Leopard
Jaguar	Bandicoot	Tiger
Giant Panda	Florida Manatee	Ocelot
Lemur	Bighorn Sheep	Blue Whale
Bobcat	Indiana Bat	Gazelle
Red Kangaroo	Sperm Whale	Silvery Gibbon

Sample interview questions: *(Be sure to add some interview questions of your own.)*

1. What is the name of your species?
2. Where do you live?
3. Has anything changed recently in your environment?
4. Have you ever been hunted by predators? If so, how did you escape?
5. How do you live? What is your typical day like?
6. Did humans have an effect on your status today?
7. Is anything being done to prevent your species from becoming extinct?
8. When did you become endangered?

How Do We Save Them?: *Endangerment Conservation Efforts*

We must save the ecosystems that animals depend on in order to exist. An **ecosystem** is a system in which all living things depend on each other for survival. The natural balance is disturbed when even one animal becomes endangered or extinct. Each cause and effect that takes place has a direct effect on some other part of the system. Several efforts have been made to save endangered species and their ecosystems.

Government agencies have passed laws to help protect animals by banning the importation and trade of many animal products. The problem is in the enforcement of these hunting regulations. The Endangered Species Act states that it is illegal to import, export, or sell wild animals across state lines. You cannot kill them or take them from the wild without a special permit. However, the lack of law enforcement and the availability of people willing to risk breaking these laws continues to have a negative effect.

Another effort to save many endangered species involves **captive breeding**. The animals are captured and then bred in zoos or animal clinics. The hope is that they will continue to breed and restore the population once they are returned to the wild. However, many of these captive animals do not thrive or reproduce once they are returned to the wild. Captive breeding is very costly and is only a last resort. It is a short-term repair that doesn't solve the original cause of endangerment, such as toxic pollution or habitat destruction. It has, however, been successful with the black-footed ferret and the California condor.

Developing wildlife refuge systems is another attempt that is being made to help save endangered animals. The goal of this attempt is to restore the natural ecosystem. Conservationists hope to preserve the habitats or homes of endangered animals. This is done through national parks, wilderness areas, and other protected habitats.

Extensive public education programs are developed by conservationists and ecologists who hope to inform people on the global extinction crisis, which is mainly due to the rapid growth and expansion of the human population. This should be a top priority for international organizations, government agencies, industry, and individuals if we hope to preserve **biodiversity** (variety of life) in the future. We must find a solution that will help human and nonhuman species live together in harmony.

Name:_____ Date:_____

How Do We Save Them?: *Endangerment Reinforcement*

To the student observer: How do we save endangered species for the future?

Analyze: What problems face mammals in your own state? What can you do to alert others to help solve these problems?

_____

_____

_____

_____

Directions: By drawing conclusions from the lesson, answer the questions below.

1. What is being done to help threatened animals recover? _____

_____

_____

_____

2. After studying endangered mammals, which ones seem to be recovering and what was done to help them?

_____

_____

_____

_____

3. What can you do to help endangered animals recover in the wild? _____

_____

_____

_____

_____

Name:_____ Date:_____

Find the Endangered Mammals: *Word Search*

To the student observer: Find and circle in the puzzle the mammals listed below. Words are printed forward, backward, horizontally, vertically, and diagonally.

```
D S I B E R I A N T I G E R Q Q V G T W T U
Z C N S U M A T O P O P P I H Y M G Y P T P
M B L A O O R A G N A K D E R H U U R N U A
N X S K C P J M R F S X K U T Y C I A H S R
P N N G I H R V U M A O F E R Y C H J U S M
X O K S U M A H K A Q F C O G K P J S O N H
E M U R U K Q M P G K M R E K E T B R C F E
G E N I R E V L O W S B P N L T X E L K L L
S M T Q V V W P P I X P T E P O C O C W O A
V Q J J A Y H O H S S Z N L A O T E B L R H
N J R T G H I Y J O S A B V N C J A A V I W
N P K S P Y P K R A C S O I A I B Z D X D E
E L A H W Y A R G I B A H N Y D P R N Y A U
J T E X I H L L R R W R T Q E N Q G A I M L
V B M V C K E F U X S F C S A A P R P X A B
H E H X L D A M Q P E U C T Y B J U T N N A
L H S M Z W E N V G J W R C E B V I N Z A R
G Q X Z N L J I S G D T Y L W J D C A N T I
T E R R E F D E T O O F K C A L B A I Q E U
D M R T R A Y X V W Z J H S J W K F G F E H
A L L I R O G N I A T N U O M A O W N X N O
N P H H D T T N I R S P G M Y F N A H Z V W
```

African Elephant

Black-footed Ferret

Florida Manatee

Lemur

Ocelot

Rhinoceros

Wolverine

Aye-Aye

Blue Whale

Giant Panda

Mountain Gorilla

Pygmy Hippopotamus

Siberian Tiger

Yak

Bandicoot

Chamois

Gray Whale

Musk Ox

Red Kangaroo

Walrus

Name:_____ Date:_____

Research: *Mammal Project*

To the student observer: Select a mammal that interests you to do a project on. After choosing your mammal, you will need to gather information about it. Your research must include at least three resources. Follow your teacher's directions for the format and length of the presentation. Your project should include the topics listed below. Use this check-off sheet to help you finish your project.

Topics:

_____   I.   Description (What it looks like)

_____   II.   Drawing or Photocopied Picture (A visual aid)

_____   III.   Classification Information (Use the chart we discussed in class.)

_____   IV.   Size Information (How big or small your mammal is)

_____   V.   Close Relatives (What other mammal is very similar to your mammal)

_____   VI.   Location and Diet (Where your mammal is found and what it eats)

_____   VII.   Behavior (How your mammal acts and why)

_____ VIII.   Life Span (How long the mammal usually lives)

_____   IX.   Reproduction

_____   X.   Conservation Facts

_____   **Extra effort:** *(Give two additional things you learned during your research).*

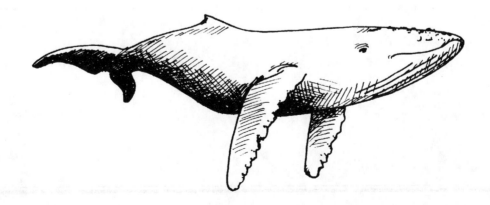

Name:_____ Date:_____

Research: *Mammal Project (cont.)*

MAMMAL: _____

I. Description: _____

_____

_____

_____

_____

_____

II. A drawing of your mammal:

Name:_____ Date:_____

Research: *Mammal Project (cont.)*

III. Classification:

Kingdom _____

Phylum _____

Class _____

Order _____

Family _____

Genus _____

Species _____

IV. Size Information: _____

_____

_____

_____

_____

V. Close Relatives Include: _____

_____

_____

_____

VI. Location and Diet: _____

Range: _____

_____

Habitat: _____

_____

_____

Diet: _____

_____

_____

Name:_____ Date:_____

Research: *Mammal Project (cont.)*

VII. Behavioral Acts: _____

_____

_____

_____

_____

_____

VIII. Life Span: _____

_____

_____

IX. Reproduction: _____

Number of offspring: _____

Gestation time: _____

X. Conservation Information and Efforts: _____

_____

_____

_____

_____

_____

Extra effort: Two other interesting facts:

_____

_____

_____

_____

_____

_____

_____

Name:_____ Date:_____

Mammal Vocabulary: *Study Sheet*

To the student observer: This is a list of important terms from the unit. Use the terms and their definitions to help you do the mammal activities in this unit. This study sheet will help you prepare for the unit test.

1. **Adaptations** - traits that help an organism survive

2. **Canines** - teeth used for tearing

3. **Carnivores** - meat-eaters

4. **Endangered** - animals that need protection in order to survive

5. **Endothermic** - warm-blooded; maintains a constant body temperature

6. **Gestation period** - amount of time it takes the embryo to develop

7. **Habitat** - area in which an animal lives

8. **Herbivores** - plant-eaters

9. **Incisors** - teeth used for biting and cutting

10. **Mammal** - a complex, warm-blooded vertebrate that has hair, nurses its young, and usually gives birth to live offspring

11. **Mammary gland** - gland that produces milk

12. **Marsupial** - pouched mammal

13. **Molars** - teeth used for grinding and crushing

14. **Monotreme** - egg-laying mammal

15. **Omnivores** - plant- and meat-eaters

16. **Organism** - a living thing

17. **Placenta** - saclike organ in which the embryo develops

18. **Placental mammal** - embryo develops inside the female mammal

19. **Poaching** - illegal hunting

20. **Range** - geographic area in which an animal lives

Name:_____   Date:_____

Mammals: *Crossword Puzzle*

To the student observer: Complete the puzzle with the information you have learned in this unit.

ACROSS
3. Warm-blooded
6. An endothermic vertebrate with hair
9. Attaches an embryo to the placenta (two words)
11. Flying mammals
12. To enter a sleep-like state during the hot months
13. Give information about the type of food eaten
17. A key that aids in the identification of organisms
19. Saclike organ in which an embryo develops
22. Most complex mammal
23. Meat-eating mammal

DOWN
1. Place where an animal usually lives
2. Illegal hunting
3. Measures distance by emitting high-pitched squeaks that bounce back as echoes
4. To enter a sleep-like state during the cold months
5. Geographic area where an animal lives
7. To change to be better suited for surroundings
8. Embryo development time
10. Mammals produce _____ offspring
14. Mammals on the move
15. Gland that produces milk
16. Pouched mammal
18. Plant-eating mammal
20. Could disappear from the earth
21. Egg-laying mammal

40

Name:_____ Date:_____

Mammals: *Unit Test*

Multiple Choice: Write the letter of the correct answer on the line at the left.

_____ 1. If an animal is a herbivore, it eats
         a. other animals.   c. other herbivores.
         b. only plants.   d. both plants and animals.

_____ 2. The group of vertebrates believed to be the most intelligent is
         a. fish.   c. mammals.
         b. birds.   d. reptiles.

_____ 3. All mammals have
         a. scales.   c. feathers.
         b. hair or fur.   d. nails.

_____ 4. Incisors are used for
         a. crushing.   c. grinding.
         b. cutting.   d. smashing.

_____ 5. Most of the marsupials in the world are found in
         a. Europe.   c. Australia.
         b. North America.   d. Asia.

_____ 6. Mammals nurse their young with milk produced in the
         a. placenta.   c. pouch.
         b. mammary glands.   d. abdomen.

_____ 7. All of the following are pouched mammals except
         a. koala bears.   c. kangaroos.
         b. opossums.   d. whales.

_____ 8. A mammal whose body temperature remains constant is called
         a. endothermic.   c. ectothermic.
         b. estivation.   d. hibernation.

_____ 9. A structure in some mammals that connects the mother with the embryo is the
         a. umbilical cord.   c. mammary gland.
         b. cusps.   d. pouch.

_____ 10. In most mammals the embryo develops
         a. inside the mother.   c. inside a pouch.
         b. inside an egg.   d. on land.

Name:_____ Date: _____

Mammals: *Unit Test (cont.)*

Matching: Put the letter of the definition in the space next to the word it matches.

_____ 1. Nocturnal   A. A scientist who studies mammals
_____ 2. Diurnal   B. To spend the cold months in a sleep-like state
_____ 3. Mammalogist   C. Where an animal normally lives
_____ 4. Poaching   D. Active at night
_____ 5. Adaptations   E. Illegal hunting
_____ 6. Habitat   F. Seasonal movement to another place
_____ 7. Echolocation   G. Active by day
_____ 8. Hibernate   H. Measuring distance by making a noise
_____ 9. Territory   I. Area an animal defends
_____ 10. Migration   J. Changes to suit the surroundings

Essay:

1. Describe the five main traits for all mammals. _____

_____

_____

_____

_____

_____

_____

_____

2. Explain why the teeth of omnivores are uniform in size. _____

_____

_____

_____

3. Compare endangered and threatened species. _____

_____

_____

_____

_____

_____

Answer Keys

What Is a Mammal?: Reinforcement Activity (page 3)

I.   MAN
     ANIMAL
     MARSUPIALS
     MAMMARY
     ALL
     LIVE OFFSPRING

II.
1. Fossils, newest
2. nurse, milk
3. vertebrae
4. endothermic
5. hair
6. cerebrums
7. therapsids
8. successful
9. specialized
10. a. vertebrate or backbone
    b. endothermic or warm-blooded
    c. produce milk in mammary glands
    d. complex brains or large cerebrums
    e. specialized teeth

Analyze: They no longer had to compete for food or a place to live. (*Food and living space are the main ideas.)

Keeping Track: Classification of Mammals Activity (page 5)

1. a. Monotremes: These mammals lay eggs in a leathery shell and incubate them.
   b. Marsupials: Marsupials are pouched mammals who give birth to offspring not fully developed. They must crawl into a pouch to finish developing.
   c. Placentals: The largest group; the embryo develops inside the mother's body until it is fully formed.

Keeping Track: Classification Review (page 6)

1. To put into groups, based on similarities
2. To make it easier to study and learn about them
3. It is a two-word naming system that gives organisms a specific name (scientific name).
4. Carolus Linnaeus
5. Write it in italics, genus name first and then species name. You must capitalize the genus name.
6. Latin
7. Taxonomy
8. Animal, plant, fungi, protists, and monera

Analyze: Answers will vary. Possible answer: Many things in our daily lives are classified to make things easier for us.

Kitchens: make food preparation easier
Libraries: make finding books easier
Grocery stores: make shopping easier
Some students may list things they classify.

Using a Dichotomous Key (page 7–8)
Procedure:

1. Lynx
   Lynx lynx

2. Mountain lion
   Puma concolor

Analyze:
1. Seven
2. Length of tail
3. Ear tufts and cheek ruffs

Conclusion:
The first pair of descriptions is the trait to divide them into the two main groups that will lead you to the correct identification. The first pair of descriptions is the most general, and each pairing thereafter is more specific. If you miss the first pairing, you could arrive at the wrong answer. (Any of these answers are acceptable.)

What's the Name?: Scientific Names (page 9)

1. *Canis latrans*
2. *Canis familiaris*
3. *Vulpes vulpes*
4. *Felis domesticus*
5. *Panthera leo*
6. *Felis concolor*
7. *Panthera tigris*
8. *Canis lupus*

Analyze: The more closely related they are, the more likely they are to be in the same genus. (Members of the same genus are very much alike.)

Conclusion: *Canis*

Mammalian Orders: Comprehension (page 18)

To the student observer: Because we are many celled, our cells are eukaryotic, we move about, we can't make our own food, and we must eat other living things.

1. Traits that help an organism survive in its environment
2. People who study mammals
3. A pouch for its young to finish developing in
4. Platypus and echidna (lay eggs)
5. Rodents
6. The beaver
7. For defense, they help them escape from predators.
8. Deer, moose, elk, caribou (any two)
9. The primates
10. Cetaceans and Sirenians make up the two orders. They live in saltwater, such as oceans and seas.

11. The bat
12. Bats make sounds that bounce back and help them locate objects. They use the sound waves to help them fly in darkness.
13. A suborder of aquatic carnivores called Pinnipeds

Problem-Solving: Echolocation (page 19)
1. Part of the sound wave is reflected back.
2. The object is located from the reflected sound wave.
3. They catch the reflected sound waves.
Analyze: They would have problems in a place that absorbs sound waves rather than reflects them.

Different Kinds of Mammals (page 20)
Examples may vary. Possible answers include:
1. Platypus
2. Kangaroo
3. Shrew
4. Bat
5. Mouse
6. Rabbit
7. Wolf
8. Deer
9. Horse
10. Elephant
11. Monkey
12. Whale
13. Manatee

Smile—Let's See Those Mammal Teeth (page 22)
To the student observer: four
1. Incisors, canines, premolars, and molars
2. Wolves have to capture and seize their prey and then tear the meat. A deer needs flatter teeth to grind its food.
3. Rodents have to gnaw through their food, so their teeth need to work like a chisel. A cow needs flat, broad teeth for chewing.
4. The incisors are in the front.
5. The elephant no longer uses its canines for chewing.
6. a. Herbivores: mammals who feed on producers or plants (strictly vegetarians)
   b. Carnivores: mammals who eat meat or feed on other animals (strictly meat-eaters)
   c. Omnivores: mammals who eat both plants and other animals
Analyze: We have all four types of teeth. We eat meat and plants, so our teeth are adapted to both types of food. We do not have any extreme teeth because we do not capture prey like a wild animal.

Mammal Teeth Activity (page 23)
A. Grazing Mammal:
1. Incisor
2. Molar
3. Premolar
4. Canine
B. Gnawing Mammal:
1. Molar
2. Premolar
3. Incisor
C. Carnivorous Mammal:
1. Incisor
2. Molar
3. Premolar
4. Canine

Food Chain Model (page 24)
Analyze: The second-order consumers in the food chain would increase in number. They would soon outnumber the first-level consumers, which is their food source. Soon, the second-order consumers would be competing for food, and they too would decline from starvation.
I. Energy, Producer, Herbivore, Carnivore, Top Carnivore
II. Student food chains will vary. Accept all logical chains.

Mammal Behavior Reinforcement (page 28)
To the student observer: Answers will vary.
Completion:
1. territorial behavior
2. Innate
3. circadian rhythm
4. behavior
5. stimuli
6. reflex
7. reasoning
8. Imprinting
Show what you know:
1. Innate and learned
2. Reflex and instinct
3. Conditioning, trial-and-error, reasoning, and imprinting
4. Sounds, facial expressions, visual displays, scents or pheromones

Endangered and Threatened: Reinforcement (page 30)
Fact/Opinion:
1. O   5. O
2. F   6. F
3. F   7. F
4. O   8. O

1. Endangered are in immediate risk of extinction and need our help to survive. Threatened are abundant in some areas and declining in others and could be at risk in the future.
2. Habitat destruction, commercial exploitation (hunted for profit), and pollution
3. Loss of habitat due to increasing human population

Analyze: Some are hunted for the products we make from them. Some become food, art objects, pets, or are sold to zoos. They are hunted for profit.

How Do We Save Them?: Endangerment Reinforcement (page 33)

Analyze: Answers will vary. Answers should indicate loss of habitat, pollution, predators, or poaching. Possible ways to alert people are writing newspaper articles and making posters or flyers to display in the community.

1. Answers will vary. Examples:
   a. Government agencies have passed laws to regulate hunting and the import and export of animals or many animal products.
   b. Captive breeding in zoos and animal clinics
   c. Wildlife refuge systems to protect ecosystems
   d. Regulation of pollution levels from industry
2. Answers will vary. Examples:
   a. Black-footed ferrets were saved by captive breeding.
   b. Elephants were saved when many countries outlawed the sale of ivory.
3. Answers will vary. Examples:
   a. Refuse to buy products made of animal parts
   b. Obey fish and wildlife conservation laws
   c. Don't pollute or hurt the environment

Find the Endangered Mammals: Word Search (page 34)

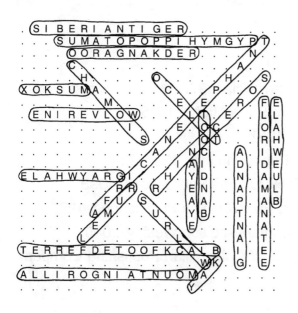

Mammals: Crossword Puzzle (page 40)

Mammals: Unit Test (pages 41–42)

Multiple Choice:	Matching:
1. b	1. D
2. c	2. G
3. b	3. A
4. b	4. E
5. c	5. J
6. b	6. C
7. d	7. H
8. a	8. B
9. a	9. I
10. a	10. F

Essay:

1. Mammals have hair or fur for insulation; some have little hair and use fat to keep them warm. They produce milk in mammary glands. They nurse and care for their young. They are endothermic or warm-blooded. Mammals have specialized teeth for the types of food they eat. They have complex brains, and most give birth to live young.
2. These mammals eat all types of food and use all their teeth equally, so their teeth are all about the same size. They do not need one type of tooth to stand out above the others.
3. Endangered animals need our protection. They are in immediate danger of extinction. Threatened species have declining numbers and may be at risk in the future.

Optional Word Banks

To the teacher: Below are word banks that may be used by the teacher with certain activities. If you have younger students or students that need a little assistance, you could let them use the word banks. Your more advanced students can work without any assistance.

Lesson: What Is a Mammal? (page 3)

fossils	animal	specialized	all	endothermic
newest	marsupial	therapsids	nurse	successful
man	mammary	live offspring	milk	cerebrum
spine	hair			

Lesson: Different Kinds of Mammals (page 20)

shrew	elephant	deer	platypus	mouse
horse	whale	bat	monkey	wolf
kangaroo	rabbit	manatee		

Lesson: Food Chain Model (page 24)

carnivore	energy	top carnivore	herbivore	producer

Lesson: Mammal Behavior—Completion (page 28)

reasoning	imprinting	behavior	territorial behavior
reflex	stimuli	innate	circadian rhythm

Lesson: Crossword Puzzle (page 40)

monotreme	adapt	placenta	mammal	dichotomous
poaching	herbivore	habitat	hibernate	endothermic
endangered	marsupial	man	migration	echolocation
carnivore	bats	range	live	umbilical cord
mammary	teeth	estivate	gestation	

Bibliography

Biggs, Daniel, and Ortleb. *Life Science.* Glencoe/McGraw-Hill, 1997.

Borton, Maurice. *Warm-Blooded Animals.* Facts On File Publications, 1985.

Carrington, Richard. *The Mammals.* Time Life Books, 1967.

Dobson, David. *Can We Save Them?* Charlesbridge Publishing Inc., 1997.

Pollock, Steve. *The Atlas Of Endangered Animals.* Facts On File Publications, 1993.

Porter, Keith. *Discovering Science/Looking At Animals.* Facts On File Publications, 1987.

Strauss, Lisowski. *The Web of Life/Biology.* Scott Foresman-Addison Wesley, 2000.

Whitfield, Philip. *Macmillan Illustrated Animal Encyclopedia.* Macmillan Publishing Company, 1984.